My

Small

Space

My Small Space

Starting Out in Style

Anna Ottum

with Chloe Lieske

Clarkson Potter/Publishers
New York

To my father, who taught us to make every house a home.

Contents

Introduction

Moving into a new place is exciting. While there's a lot to consider when choosing the right spot, that's only the first of the decisions you'll make. Now you're faced with the fun of figuring out how to put it all together. You might be dreaming about decorating your bedroom, searching for layout inspiration, or looking forward to entertaining friends. Whether you're sharing an apartment or dorm with roommates or signing the lease on your first studio, living in a small space has its own challenges and possibilities.

I grew up in a very eclectic home. My father has always loved interior design and is constantly experimenting with different looks, redecorating rooms on a whim. As a result, I was encouraged to see my spaces as an expression of myself and used them to develop my own personal style. Even when I was barely making enough money to cover the necessities, I always found ways to make a place feel special.

Over the past few years, I've been invited to photograph many fun and cool homes. Each one was a reflection of the people who lived there—their personalities, interests, values, and lifestyles. I loved learning about the occupants through the stories their spaces told: the origin of a special object or the inspiration behind a collection of art. Sometimes a book would offer a glimpse into someone's guilty pleasure, or a single piece of furniture would open up a whole story about how they grew up.

This book includes many of those creative spaces: co-designed lofts, tiny dorm rooms, and compact studios—all organized by communal, campus, and solo setups. Although they represent a wide range of aesthetic sensibilities (from modern and minimal to colorful and collected), every place offers a unique take on space-conscious design, some feature open floor plans and low-maintenance layouts while others highlight smart storage solutions and multi-functional furniture.

There's also lots of practical advice—like how to negotiate roommate conflicts, tips on setting up budgets and cleaning schedules, what to pack for college, and the best way to work with a real estate agent—as well as decorating ideas for choosing the right rug, hanging a gallery wall, and picking the perfect paint color.

Wherever and however you choose to live, I hope that you're inspired to experiment, take risks, and find your own small space style, ultimately creating a home of your own—and one that you love.

Communal

When you're just starting out, living with roommates is an obvious choice. Not only will you have built-in buddies and help with the cleaning, but you'll also be able to pool your money for a better place than you would get on just one income, especially in cities where salaries don't rise as fast as the rents. Despite the challenges of learning to work with a housemate's quirks and pet peeves, many people love the sense of community that co-living creates. Whether you're looking with friends, a significant other, a sibling, or strangers, sharing a space means finding common ground.

Planning
Pick Your Partners Carefully.

Good friends don't always make good roommates, and good roommates don't always make good friends. Someone who's fun to hang out with might not be the most conscientious housemate and vice versa. Consider how much time you each spend at home and how often it will overlap. Do you like having people over? Will someone be using the living room as a home office?

If you decide not to live with friends, always ask people you trust for recommendations as well as looking at listings online. You never know who has a spare room or knows of one that's opening up. And meet any potential candidates in person. Even if you've done your due diligence, compatibility can be hard to gauge over text or email—ultimately, go with your gut.

Connect over common interests. It's easy to bond when you have similar tastes or hobbies, like a love of music— especially if you're both homebodies. Bonus: merging your things in the common spaces will be easier.

Come together. You might get lucky and double your living room's record collection or expand your library. Even if your belongings don't totally mesh, know that contrast in design is a good thing. Highlight—rather than hide—your differences and unique interests.

ASK A ROOMMATE FINDER

AJAY YADAV, ROOMI, THE ROOMMATE REFERRAL APP

How does Roomi ensure that people find good roommates? Our vision is to create a community for shared living so that your house always feels like a home. Our app allows users the options of background checks, full ID verification, in-app messaging, and secure rent payments to help build safety and trust. We take the search very seriously and match people based on compatibility: Are you a night owl or an early riser? A party animal or a gym rat?

When is the right time to start looking for a roommate? Even though the search process (from signing up to booking a room) usually lasts about ten days, we recommend talking to potential roommates even earlier so you're not waiting until the last minute to make a decision.

Any advice for someone who is looking for a roommate for the first time? Focus more on finding the right person than finding the right place. Everyone has a specific budget in mind and once you narrow down where you can afford to live, you should spend most of your time and energy looking for the right roommate. Your first experience living with someone else will set the tone for future setups.

How do you feel about living with friends versus strangers?

Personally, I'm fine with either, but I like to try new experiences—so if I had to choose, I'd probably live with a stranger. I've mostly lived with strangers and have had very different and unique experiences each time.

What five questions should you always ask a potential roommate?

1. What's your sleep schedule? Do you stay up late or go to bed early?
2. What about parties? Do you like having lots of people over or prefer to go out?
3. Find out if there are any activities they're into. For example, I always ask if they like to bike or go for walks because that might be something we can do together.
4. What are your cleaning habits? It's good to make sure you're living with someone who can tidy up after themselves.
5. Another good way to find common interests is to ask about their favorite movie. I like watching science fiction so it's nice to know if they're into that, too.

Once you move in together, how do you maintain a good living situation?

Set house rules at the beginning and follow them. I'd focus on things that you really care about—for me, that would be splitting expenses equally, paying bills on time, cleaning up after yourself, and respecting personal space (I like to lay in on Sunday mornings without disturbance until at least nine a.m.).

Do you have any tips on setting up a space and decorating with a new roommate? What if you have different tastes?

I like different! I usually like to brainstorm ideas together. Get everyone involved early on so you can think about decorating as a team. Maybe even plan a few group outings: browsing design stores (and sites online), spending the afternoon at an art gallery, or visiting furniture or fabric showrooms are all great ways to get inspired.

On average, how often do people change roommates?

With Roomi, we're seeing that people stay in a place for around 6 months. People seem to be moving more often, from city to city.

If a roommate situation isn't working out, how do you recommend making a graceful exit?

Come up with a process together and try to be as transparent as possible. Set a move-out date, inform everyone in good time, and look for someone else to replace you as soon as possible.

Find inspiration everywhere. From going to flea markets to leafing through magazines, spend time looking for decorating ideas together. Think about how you want to design your apartment and talk about ways to display your things so that you both feel at home. Use white walls to your advantage: it's a clean backdrop for disparate art and objects. Consider adding a bright accent color to tie collections together.

Follow the rainbow. Use color as an organizing principle to take a mix of things from chaotic to collected. By stacking and leaning books together, loosely based on palette, two (or more) roommates' volumes come together in one cohesive library. A bright bookcase adds a bold frame.

Secrets to Living with a Significant Other

So you've decided to move in together. You're about to be closer than ever and learn things you never knew about your partner. First, decide on where you'll live —sometimes a new place is best because there isn't an imbalanced sense of ownership and you can start fresh as a couple. Here are some things to consider when you're cohabiting.

Assess your stuff.

Since you'll be building a new home and your individual storage space will shrink, it's important to look at what you both have and decide what to keep and what to get rid of—you don't want to bring literal baggage into your new apartment.

Combine your tastes.
It's exciting to style a joint space. Discuss your decorating goals and come up with a plan. Even if one of you is more invested, talk through the big decisions to make sure nothing is a deal breaker.

Talk about it.
Money. Bad habits. Things that get under your skin. Good communication is key. Be open and honest about things upfront so you don't get into arguments or passive-aggressive standoffs later on.

Learn to compromise.
You're in this together. Lay out your expectations—like how much time you need to get ready on a workday or how long you can deal with dirty dishes in the sink—and come to an agreement on how you'll share responsibilities and merge your routines.

Allow for alone time.
You might be used to retreating to your room when you want to be by yourself, but now it belongs to both of you. Respect each other's privacy when one of you needs some space.

My Small Space

Communal

Get the hang of it.
Installing art on a wall can be tricky, but it's easier with a second set of hands. As a general rule, give pieces room to breathe and line them up at about eye level (approximately 57 inches from the ground). Some people like to align the tops of each frame while others choose the center—but you can mix it up, too.

Short on shelves? Stack books on the floor, on a coffee table, or next to a sofa in place of a side table. Not only will they put your interests on display, but you'll also ensure that any leisure reading is always within arm's reach.

TIPS FOR TOUGH CONVER– SATIONS

It's not always easy to talk about things that are bothering you— whether it's a roommate who always has people over without notice or a partner who never picks up after themself. Here's how to make your needs clear without coming off as uptight.

Bring things up early.
As soon as you feel tensions rise, it's time to talk about the issue.

Talk face to face.
Don't have important conversations over email or text. Body language and facial expressions add so many emotional nuances that are hard to pick up and easy to misinterpret if you're not sitting in front of each other.

Keep it casual.
Meet somewhere neutral, like a quiet café, where you're both comfortable but still have some privacy.

Be empathetic.
Try to understand where the other person is coming from. It's good practice to focus more on what you're hearing than on what you're saying. If you feel yourself getting worked up, take a break and continue the conversation later on.

Compromise . . . or don't.
Know when something is a deal breaker for you—especially with a significant other. If they love and respect you, they'll be willing to accommodate.

Adulting

Set Some Boundaries.

It's a good idea to create a few
house rules so you can all live
together without getting under
each other's skin. You might
make a roommate agreement,
spelling out things like how
often a boyfriend or girlfriend
can spend the night, how
cleaning duties will be divide,
and when it's okay to have
groups of people over or throw
a party. These contracts aren't
binding, of course, but they
include the kinds of details
that can make or break your
day-to-day.

Figure Out Finances.

Decide how you'll split expenses before you sign the lease to help avoid some awkward conversations later on. Either assign each bill to a different person or elect one roommate to handle all of them and use a spreadsheet to split up the total at the end of each month. Another way to keep things even is to start a petty cash jar. If everyone chips in a few dollars a week, there should be enough to replace toilet paper, lightbulbs, and cleaning products in a pinch.

Co-design Your Space.

Chances are you and your roommates won't have identical tastes when it comes to decorating. You can style your bedroom however you want, but you'll have to compromise when it comes to the common areas. Take a quick inventory of what everyone already has and decide what to keep, sell, donate, or throw out. Then figure out what you need to buy together. Discuss whether each person will be responsible for one big purchase or if you'll split the total evenly and work out who gets what when you eventually move on. Either way, try to respect each other's tastes and budgets.

Communal

Don't be a basket case.
Even if you're not a neat
freak, there are plenty
of messy-clean and quick
solutions to staying
organized. Think like with
like—a basket on the floor
lets you throw hats or
totes together without
having to overthink it as
you're walking in the door.

**Ask about outdoor
areas.** When space is
limited, especially in cities
where you won't have a big
backyard—roof access or
a shared garden can add
precious square feet.

Leave a message. Clear communication is extra important if you don't spend a lot of time at home together. An oversize chalkboard can become an easy tool for leaving notes and reminders for roommates: things the super needs to fix, grocery lists, or a simple heads-up about out-of-town guests. If you like to entertain, use the space to play games like hangman or Pictionary.

Hold everything. Use a trunk instead of a traditional coffee table for extra storage—it's great for stowing blankets and spare bedding for when friends crash overnight.

Lighting is one of the easiest ways to make a difference in your space. The goal isn't to make everything as bright as possible, but rather to create contrast and depth with a warm mix that you can adjust based on mood and time of day. Here's how to make your place shine.

Look overhead.

Rental-appointed fixtures tend to be harsh and lackluster. If you can, replace them with something softer. Dimmers also make a difference—try a plug-in style or ask if your landlord or super can help install them for a little extra cash.

Increase your sources.

A single, central ceiling light can make a space feel flat. Sprinkle light sources around the room at different levels to make it seem larger and more inviting.

Play with scale.

Floor lamps make use of empty space and add height to a seating area, while table lamps provide pockets of warmth on side tables, bookshelves, and consoles.

Find the right angles.

Make sure to spotlight desks and bedsides in a way that doesn't have you working or reading in your own shadow—and use 60-watt bulbs so you don't strain your eyes.

Light candles.

Candles dotted around a room can have a dramatic effect. Battery-operated or LED votives are good options because you can leave them on for long periods of time.

Greenery adds life to a space, has a calming effect (like being outside in nature), and even improves air quality by releasing oxygen and absorbing carbon dioxide. Some plants almost take care of themselves, while others require a bit more maintenance. Here's how to get things growing.

Pick the right plants.
Always buy healthy insect-free plants with strong leaves and firm stems. Different plants have different needs so consider the conditions in your apartment before making any purchases. If you're not sure, pothos, aloe, ivy, and rubber trees are especially resilient. Some plants are toxic to cats and dogs, so ask questions or research online if you have pets.

Watch how you water.
Yellow-tipped leaves are a good indication that plants need less moisture while droopy leaves let you know they need more. Generally, soil for houseplants should be damp but not soggy—and make sure pots have drainage holes so water doesn't stand around roots and cause rotting.

Give them light.
How much natural light does your apartment get? While every plant needs the sun, the degrees of direct and filtered light vary. Do some research to help figure out what to pick and where to put it. Plants take a while to acclimate to new locations, so try not to move them too often.

Keep them clean.
Dust can block sunlight so give your plants a shower every now and then or wipe large leaves with a damp cloth.

Know when to re-pot.
If plants start drying out faster than usual, water runs through the soil quickly, or you see roots poking out of the drainage holes, it's probably time to re-pot. Increase a pot's diameter by only an inch or two, and always use fresh potting soil since nutrients deplete over time.

Create a hanging garden. Even if it turns out that you have less floor space than you think and most of your shelves and tabletops are taken over with other things, it doesn't mean you can't have plants. Hanging them in or near a window is a smart way to give them unobstructed light and fill otherwise unused space. Try installing curtain rods or a beam—and look for inexpensive macramé or woven hangers on craft sites such as Etsy. Just know that plants are much heavier once they've been watered, so make sure whatever rod you use can handle the weight.

Communal

Organizing

Get It Together.

A well-appointed apartment has the power to affect your well-being. Some psychologists say that a cluttered space can make you feel scattered and anxious. Since rentals rarely come with enough closets and you likely won't have a basement to store things out of site, find creative ways to minimize mess with multi-functional furniture and accessories. Keeping things in order helps maintain your sense of calm.

Find the perfect fit. An odd-shaped table fills the small nook between a bed and the wall, extending a deep windowsill to allow space for a few art objects as well as bedside necessities.

More people means more stuff. A shared space has the tendency to get chaotic quickly so it's important to assign a spot for everyone's belongings. Once you know where things go, set up a cleaning schedule to keep things tidy. Here's how to stay organized.

Learn to multitask. Pieces with more than one purpose are game-changing in a small space. For example, use a trunk with storage as a coffee table or put a filing cabinet next to a sofa so that it can double as a side table.

Go modular. Flexible furniture—like shelving units you can add onto, boxes that stack, and chairs that fold—means it's easy to create more storage as you need more space.

Make the most of bookshelves. Boxes, baskets, and trays contain clutter on open shelving. They also visually break up rows of books and add dimension.

Use dressers outside of the bedroom. Chests of drawers provide prime storage all over the house. They come in all kinds of sizes and finishes—think about using one that's low and wide as a TV stand or a more compact shape in an entryway.

Maximize accessories. Decorative boxes, bowls, and baskets are attractive ways to conceal receipts, notebooks, and other knickknacks.

Make every surface count. Look for unexpected or traditionally unused spaces: the tops of kitchen cabinets can hold bottles or display art; a freestanding kitchen island provides storage in the middle of the room; and a thin shelf under a television acts like a streamlined console.

Seek out middle ground. Putting all of your furniture against the walls can create a cluttered vibe. Try floating pieces—like a large sofa or sectional—in the room's interior, to create an airy look that keeps walls and windows accessible.

Privacy, please. Loft spaces are fun, but add a roommate, and you'll soon want some space. No worries: Use a large cabinet or shelving unit to divide an open area into a bedroom and a living area. To make it feel less like floating furniture and more like a built-in, try painting the back of the bookshelf white (or match it to the color of your room), so it acts as a wall on one side and storage for books and objects on the other.

Get creative. If you can't find the furniture you're looking for, consider commissioning a handy friend or relative to build something for you. A custom lofted bed with plywood cubbies is the ideal situation for a small space, providing shelves for books and records and drawers for clothes and blankets. A clever hollow staircase adds even more spots to store things.

Gather Around.

Entertaining can be so much fun when you're living with friends; just make sure everyone's on the same page when planning a get-together. Take schedules into account, agree on how many people to invite, and delegate duties so that they play to people's strengths— or take turns planning the menu, making the playlist, and decorating the living room. If you entertain often, consider starting a "party pool" each month to help cover the cost of food and drinks. And definitely take your friends up on their offers to bring snacks and drinks.

Listen to the music. The right tunes play a huge part in setting a mood or creating a vibe. If you're having a get-together, encourage everyone to participate in the playlist. Make it a social activity by keeping records accessible so friends can take turns throwing on their favorite album or song whenever they want.

Home Bar Essentials

When cocktails are too expensive or the bar is too far, make your own drinks at home with a few simple ingredients. If you don't have room for a bar cart, a section of a bookshelf or a tray in the kitchen will do the trick. A well-stocked bar should be built over time. Here's how to get started.

Begin with the basics.
You don't need every kind of booze at first. A decent bottle of whiskey, vodka, gin, rum, and tequila, plus sweet vermouth and Angostura bitters is enough to make plenty of different cocktails.

Add a few mixers.
Have small cans of ginger ale or ginger beer, soda, and tonic on hand—they're perfectly portioned for one or two drinks.

Get the right gear.
You can get away with very few tools, but you should have a shaker, a mixing glass, a strainer, a stirring spoon, and a jigger for measuring.

Collect your glasses.
Certain glasses are made to enhance a drink, but you don't need every shape and style. Just make sure you have a mix of sizes: smaller for sipping and larger for tall drinks with lots of ice.

Keep it cool.
Don't underestimate the power of good ice—it's a key ingredient that will affect flavor. Always make sure ice is fresh and pieces are large enough so they don't melt too fast and water down your drink.

Have an extra seat. Experiment with unconventional seating arrangements that help maximize a small space. A console can double as a bench—just throw down a folded blanket to make a soft cushion. Or use a chair to hold any nighttime necessities—you'll be more than happy to have an extra reading nook.

Campus

Heading to college is one of the biggest changes you'll experience in your life. It might be the first time you're away from home and your family, or you might be moving to a different city, state, even country. Living the campus life presents its own set of challenges and opportunities—balancing school and maybe work with new friends and fun. Setting up a space you love will help set you up for success.

Moving

Congrats! You're On Your Own.

It's tiny and bathroom-less and you're sleeping three feet away from a stranger. Welcome to your dorm room. Working with limited storage and school-sanctioned furniture might seem uninspiring, but amping up an underwhelming space just takes a few personal touches. Start with a cozy bed, then add photos, posters, plants, and lighting to tailor your room to your personality. Working around a set of rules and restrictions only forces you to be more creative.

An object lesson:
Carve out little spaces for mementoes and personal items to remind you of home—and leave room for new memories, too. A small ledge above your desk is a natural spot for a few photos, figurines, and bottles. And a deep windowsill near the bed doubles as a nightstand and a place to display special collections.

Make blanket statements. A cozy dorm room starts with a comfy bed. Pile on the pillows, throws, and blankets and play with prints and textures to make the space feel especially inviting. Continue the homey vibes with a canape, string lights, and even a soft rug for hanging out.

ASK AN RA

KATIE GAROFALO, RESIDENT ADVISER AT SKIDMORE COLLEGE

Walk us through your role as an RA. We don't like to use the word "dorm" where I go to school because it can have a cold connotation. Instead, we call them "res-halls" to remind students that there is supposed to be residential life happening there. My role is to help make the res-hall a space that people feel comfortable in and somewhere that can approximate the feeling of coming home at the end of a long day. We build spaces of community and respect by organizing fun community building events and raising awareness of issues such as alcoholism and mental health.

What are the best things about dorm life? It's a small space so there's not much cleaning and your friends are all around you or just a short walk away. The space is cozy and easy to customize. It's really nice to walk into an empty white room and adapt it however you're feeling that year, and next year you can change it up because you'll have another brand-new canvas.

The biggest challenges? Roommate disagreements come up a lot in shared rooms. Another problem is not being able to cook for yourself. But the biggest challenge I see is homesickness. Many find it hard to see their new room as a home, especially if they don't put much effort into decorating or making it feel personal.

What items do you recommend that students bring with them to the dorms? What should they leave at home? Bring big comfy pillows in fun colors and designs, fuzzy blankets, lots of plants, twinkle lights, objects and knickknacks from your own bedroom, and pictures of family and pets. Leave behind tapestries, hot plates, candles, incense, extension cords, microwaves, and curtains.

Any tips for moving day? Spend as much time as possible decorating because if you don't start the first day, it probably won't happen. Meet your RA and neighboring suitemates since you'll be seeing these people a lot, and starting out with good relationships will help make the transition easier. Keep your parents around for as long as they can stay, and let them help you make the room feel like home. My mom always helps me decorate my room, and it really makes me feel like I have a good start to the year.

Do you have any tricks for making a small space personal, especially when there are certain restrictions?

Since many rooms come with bright fluorescent lighting, twinkle lights are great and provide warm, cozy light. I like to decorate my walls with photos (FreePrints is a great photo printing app), and I've found that tack works best for keeping them up. The bedspread is usually the main focal point in a room, so pick one wisely and layer with decorative pillows and blankets. Plants are another favorite way to decorate. One of my friends bought a suspension rod and put it in the cubby over her window seat to hang glass planters—it was so pretty.

How do you entertain in a dorm room?

Get on the same level. When I host, we all sit on the floor. Have lots of board games in your room and plenty of mugs and cups. This is always the thing no one plans for, but when you host, everyone should have a drink. I don't like to use plastic cups because they don't make the place feel like home. Turn on the twinkle lights but keep music low—the sound from your phone speaker should be enough to create some atmosphere.

Do you have guidelines for getting along with your new roommates?

Set up boundaries from the beginning. I always hand out a sheet on the first day for roommates to discuss their expectations upfront. It includes questions like: Do you see your room as a community space or a space to sleep? What is the vibe you want to come back to? Are you okay with people in your room? Are you okay with borrowing stuff? What are your goals for the year? What are your goals for your relationship with your roommate (acquaintance, friend, best friend)? Most residents completely ignore it, but almost all of them come to me later with issues that were mentioned and could have been prevented.

What are the best ways to resolve conflicts?

Use your RA as a resource to mediate. Conflict resolution starts with a neutral third party. I like to tell students that I am Switzerland, and whether they are America or North Korea, I am impartial and will help find common ground and a solution to the disagreement.

If you could give new students one piece of advice, what would it be?

Your dorm won't feel like a home until you feel at home at your school. That means you need to be active in campus and residential life—get a job, join clubs, hang out with friends, make college life your life while you're there. Once you feel at home at your school, your dorm should fall in line.

The Rules of Engagement

You're probably not used to having someone in your personal space all the time—let alone someone you just met. Even if you don't become best friends, getting along with your new roommate will make the adjustment easier. Here's how to start out on the right foot.

Call first. Give your roommate a ring before moving day so you can get to know each other and work out who's bringing the TV and who's bringing the mini fridge. You could even see if they're interested in choosing a color scheme for the room so your bedding coordinates.

Get good at communicating. Don't let problems linger. Have an honest conversation about any issues as soon as they come up.

Keep it clean. A small space can feel cluttered quickly, so set up a cleaning schedule early on and try to stick to it.

Respect each other. Accommodate each other's need for privacy and alone time. You might even agree to avoid hosting friends or playing loud music on certain nights.

Find some perspective. There's a good chance you and your roommate won't see eye to eye on everything— you may have different sleeping and study habits or opposing thoughts on politics and religion. Trying to understand each other's point of view will make it easier to communicate.

Check All the Boxes. Study the list of what your school provides and what you can and can't move from home. Most schools won't let you bring in large furniture, appliances like toasters and microwaves, candles, or window air conditioners. Here are a few must-haves for any college dorm:

· Twin XL sheets
· Mattress pad
· Sleep mask
· Lap desk
· Shower caddy/tote
· Mini fridge
· Noise-canceling headphones

Coordinate, coordinate. In such tight quarters, you don't want to waste precious space. Talk to your new dormmate before you move in and be clear about who's bringing what so you don't end up with two coffee pots. It's also a good idea to discuss anything you need to pick up that will make your room feel homey, like lamps or curtains.

Transform Your Dorm.

You'll be spending a lot of time sleeping, studying, and hanging out in one small space—so make the most of it. Try on different looks and get creative with decor: Consider temporary tricks like using colorful washi tape to frame photos, adding string lights or task lamps for ambiance, and playing with throws, rugs, and floor cushions to layer on some warmth. Think about it as a low-commitment opportunity to experiment with your personal style. If you end up not liking the look, or if you get tired of it, you can easily replace items or start over completely.

Let it shine. Bring your dorm to life with a wall of photos, posters and prints. Since you may not be able to make holes in the walls, use tack or washi tape to hang things up. Start with things from your bedroom at home and then add new pieces as the year goes on. String lights add tons of ambiance and are a great alternative to unpleasant overhead fixtures.

A Crash Course in Color Theory

Color can make a room look bigger or smaller. It can make you feel calm or energized. Some say certain colors can even make you more or less productive. Understanding the impact of hues will help you pull together palettes and make better decorating decisions. Here's how to set the tone.

Warm up. Reds, oranges, and yellows have longer wavelengths and are said to "leap out" at the viewer, stimulating the mind.

Stay cool. Blue and violet have shorter wavelengths. They usually recede and have a relaxing effect.

Go green. These shades fall in the middle of the spectrum and tend to make you feel more restful since your eyes don't need to adjust very much to see them.

Stay neutral. White, gray, and black combine well with almost any color. Black is said to decrease the brightness of adjacent colors, while white doesn't alter a shade.

Be complementary. Colors opposite from each other on the color wheel—blue and orange, red and green, yellow and purple, are complementary. Using these together in a range of shades is a good place to start when you're picking accent pieces. For example, pair pale apricot and bright orange pillows with a sea-blue duvet.

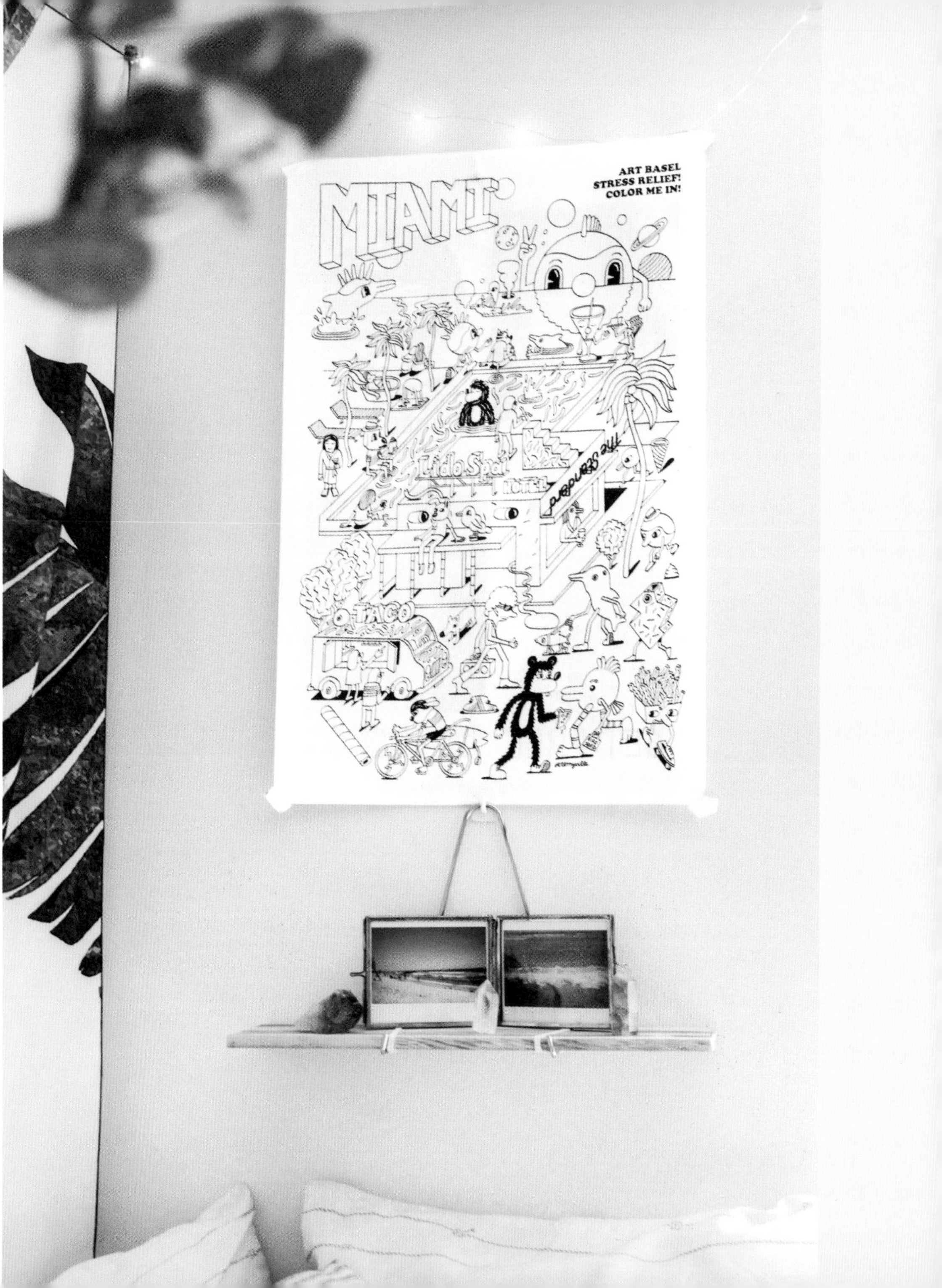
ART BASEL
STRESS RELIEF!
COLOR ME IN!
MIAMI
Lido Spa
TACO

Go green and graphic. Posters and plants are low-maintenance, high-impact ways to make a statement in your dorm. Flyers and concert posters tend to be bigger, making it easy to cover large areas—almost like wallpaper. A few plants add instant life. Try growing a small herb garden and you'll have garnishes for drinks and extra flavor for lackluster cafeteria meals.

Make some noise. Then cancel it out. Talk to your roommate about when and where to take phone calls, when it's okay to play music, and when you need quiet time. Noise-canceling headphones are a good investment if you don't always agree.

A Cheat Sheet to Not Making Your Bed

Most designers agree that a made bed helps reduce visual clutter, especially in a small space. But when the daily bustle gets in the way, the right layers can make it look even better unmade. Think ultimate bedhead for your bed. Here's how to get that lived-in look.

Stick with a soft color palette. While it can be fun to experiment with patterned sheets and bright colors, a carefree look should be totally toned down. Skip too much contrast and seek out a soft color that you like—whether blush pink, charcoal, or light beige—then riff off of it with variations on the same theme.

Get a feel for sheets you love. You'll want a fitted and a flat sheet in a material that's soft to the touch. Remember that thread count can be deceiving, so read online reviews and really do your research. Egyptian and pima cotton are good options.

Stack up the pillows. You need more than two pillows: try a queen pillow in front of a Euro sham (great for leaning against while you're studying), plus a decorative pillow or two (no more than that—this is not your grandma's house).

Add lots of texture. This is what's going to give your bed the loft that it needs to look good, whether it's made or unmade. Depending on your budget, try at least one layer in 100 percent linen. Linen is to bedding as sea salt spray is to hair: it's the best shortcut to texture and holds its shape long after you slip out of bed.

Toss in a throw. Think chunky knits at the foot of your bed for additional color and texture. The more casual looking, the better.

My Small Space

Work it out. If you're able to loft your bed, set up the space underneath as a work area. A simple screen becomes a place where you can display things you're working on, pin up inspiration, and leave little notes and reminders for yourself.

Make Pieces Work Harder.

When you can't bring in furniture and space is tight, the pieces you have need to multitask. Your room may not have a sofa, so your bed is not only where you sleep, but also one of the only places to sit. A desk might be the largest surface area in the room, so keeping it clutter-free means it's easier to turn it into a makeshift coffee bar. Get inventive with accessories, too—an empty upside-down wastebasket can become a side table and a stool can transform into extra seating.

79

Campus

The Many Uses of an Electric Kettle

The dining hall can feel miles away when you're starving, so set up a snack station right in your room. Even though you don't have an oven and most appliances aren't allowed, an electric kettle is surprisingly versatile. Here's how to get cooking.

Brew coffee. Pour-over coffee is easy and efficient when you just want a single cup. Put a filter in a ceramic or plastic coffee dripper set over a mug and fill the filter about halfway with grounds. Then slowly pour hot water in a circular motion over them until enough coffee strains through and fills your mug.

Boil an egg. Get your protein in a pinch. Put eggs in the bottom of the kettle and add water to cover them by about two inches. When the water boils, turn it off and let them sit for fifteen minutes. Then drain the eggs and put them in a bowl of cold water until they're cool enough to peel.

Cook oatmeal.
This works for lunch and dinner, too. Cover a half cup of instant oats (enough for a single portion) with just under a cup of boiling water and let sit until the oats puff up. After they cool down a bit, you can add toppings like fruit or yogurt. Try a savory version by adding olive oil, grated cheese, and greens or fresh herbs.

Make ramen. Pour hot water over noodles and let them sit for about three minutes. Then up your noodle game by swapping out the packaged spices for a scoop of miso paste and adding a handful of cooked veggies from the food hall.

81

Living by yourself is a rite of passage. Once you've navigated the listings and negotiated with a landlord, your space is all yours. No one will keep you up at night, hog the bathroom in the morning, or drink the last beer in the fridge. As much fun as it can be to live with friends, eventually keeping a shower schedule and negotiating who's going to take out the trash gets old. Even the best communal living situations have an expiration date. It's finally time to get your own place.

Moving
Do What
You Want.

For most people transitioning from living with others, a studio apartment is the natural next step. It's minimal space to furnish and generally more affordable than a one bedroom. You may think you won't be able to make so little a space work or that being able to see your kitchen from your bed isn't for you, but with an efficient layout and personal touches, a tiny space can have tons of style.

Finding the Right Rug

A quality rug provides soundproofing and adds warmth and texture to a space. Rugs are often expensive so think of them as investment pieces. Use your style and set-up to guide you toward the perfect textile. Here are a few ground rules.

Size things up. The layout you choose will help determine what size rug works best. As a general rule, if your sofa is against a wall, the rug should sit under its front legs; if the sofa is floating in the middle of the room, your rug should be large enough to fit under all four legs; and for dining rooms, the rug should extend about 2 feet on each side of the table. Smaller runners are great for hallways, entryways, and on either side of a bed.

Find your style. You might gravitate toward natural fibers like jute and sisal for their durable, easygoing feel. Flat-woven rugs like kilims and dhurries are reversible and easy to clean, while tufted rugs have more depth and softness but tend to be a little more difficult to care for.

Pick a pattern or palette. Rugs usually cover large areas and have a big impact. Let bright colors and bold patterns set the tone for a space, or use a neutral solid to ground busier patterns elsewhere in the room.

Think about traffic patterns. Avoid light-colored rugs in entryways and kitchens where people pass through often so you don't have to worry about frequent cleaning.

Experiment with layers. If you stick to a cohesive palette, layering multiple rugs can create an eclectic, multidimensional effect.

Build character. Many people seek out the charm of older houses and apartment buildings with decorative details and moldings. You might not have every amenity, like an elevator or central air, but you'll have a unique space that you can tailor to your taste. Work with built-ins such as mantels and other nooks and crannies to create unexpected storage and display areas—like a plant at the foot of a staircase or records stacked in a nonworking fireplace.

A Primer on Paints

Be sure to check your lease carefully, but most landlords don't mind if you paint as long as you go with something relatively neutral—or return it to the way it was when you leave. Finding the perfect color can be overwhelming when you're flipping through hundreds of hues. Here's how to make every coat count.

Let the light guide you.
Natural light plays a huge part in how colors change from one spot to another—determining which ways your windows face will clue you in. South-facing rooms make most colors look brighter. North-facing rooms generally get the least light and make colors feel cooler. East-facing rooms get lots of light in the morning, which works well with warmer shades. West-facing rooms get their best light in the evening, and their low morning light can make some colors look dull.

Always test first.
Painting is hard work so you want to do it only once. Before you buy a gallon, invest in a one-pint sample pot of each color you want to try. Paint a few swatches on the wall and see how the color looks during the day and the evening. If you don't want to make a bunch of marks while you experiment, paint a square of foam or poster board and tape it up to see how it looks. You might even move the board around the room so you can understand how the color changes in different lighting.

Find the right finish.
Once you've picked the perfect shade, you need to choose a finish. Flat and matte paints reflect less light and don't draw attention to small imperfections. The downside is that they're more difficult to clean. Eggshell and satin paints provide a subtle sheen, like the surface of an egg, and are easy to wipe down.

Don't forget to prime.
While it's tempting to just go for it, a primer covers walls more easily than new paint and prevents the need to apply an extra coat.

might be things that new renters don't think about. If you're working with a broker or agent, you have someone advocating on your behalf.

What are five questions you should always ask before choosing someone to work with?

1. What percentage of your clients are renters versus landlords?
2. In which neighborhoods do you primarily work? How familiar are you with the neighborhoods I'm interested in?
3. Will I be working with you directly? Do you work full-time or part-time as an agent?
4. How many other clients are you representing right now? How many landlords? (The busiest agents are often the most efficient.)
5. Can you provide names and phone numbers of past clients who have agreed to be references? (Insights from past customers can help you learn more about an agent and give you a greater comfort level.)

Are there fees involved? If you're hiring or agreeing to work with an agent, you'll generally be paying them 15% of the annual rent. Sometimes this can be negotiated down to 12% or one month's rent. In addition to the agent's fee, you generally need to pay the landlord a month's security along with the first month's rent.

What makes a great apartment? Condition, space, light, location, and access to public transportation.

ASK A BROKER

LAURA HESS,
REALTOR AT CORCORAN

Why use a real estate agent?
I highly recommend working with a real estate agent if you're looking for the first time. Many people aren't familiar with the process, and there can be a lot of scams out there. Sometimes the euphoria of getting your first apartment can cloud your judgment, and there

If it has amazing views but it's a fourth-floor walkup, are the four floors worth it? Always test the faucets and take a look in the cabinets and drawers. Watch who's coming in and out of the building and take a good look at the neighborhood. Public transportation is a big one—an apartment might be beautiful with lots of amenities, but if you're 25 minutes from transportation, your daily commute is going to cost you more time. And time is money.

How about a great landlord?
Communication and availability. There will always be issues with the property from time to time. Most of these will be small in nature, but that doesn't mean they should be ignored. Whatever comes up, both a good landlord and the tenant need to know who to contact.

Are there any red flags to look out for?
There are misleading photos and listing descriptions that stretch the truth. You always have to see a place in person. If it seems too good to be true, it probably is. If you walk into the lobby and there's paint peeling off the walls or broken steps, it means the landlord isn't present or taking very good care of the building. Make sure to ask lots of questions if you have any reservations—an agent will find out the answers to the best of their ability. And look at sites like PropertyShark, where you can see any complaints from past residents.

How do you know when you've found the right place?
I think you know when you walk into a space and it's in your price range and all of the stars are aligned. You don't need to see tons of properties, but if you have certain things that you're looking for (pet-friendly, doorman, dishwasher, outdoor space, etc.), then you might want to check out a few places before making a decision. Typically, people see five to ten, and some see more. It all depends on your timeline and when you need to move.

What kinds of changes are allowed?
Usually a landlord will let you do what you want to an apartment as long as you return it to the state it was when you initially rented it. Just remember, black paint is very hard to cover and could cost you your security deposit. Always communicate with your landlord about any improvements or changes you want to make. If they ultimately make the apartment better, your landlord most likely won't have an issue with them.

Will my rent increase?
It's a free market, and unless you've found a rent-stabilized apartment, a landlord is free to raise the rent at whatever rate they want. Usually they won't unless they want you to move out. If you're a good tenant, you can always negotiate. Say your landlord wants to raise your rent $100, ask if they can work with you and raise it $50 instead. If they have to relist the apartment and it's vacant for a month, they'll oftentimes end up losing more. In the end, it's all about math.

Solo

A Key to Listing Lingo

House hunting is hard—especially when you have to learn a whole new vocabulary that's filled with confusing euphemisms. Here are a few terms and red flags to look out for when you're looking for a place.

Alcove Studio: A studio that has an alcove, usually large enough to fit a bed. Although this space isn't separated by a door, it can help create separation between living and sleeping areas.

Application Fee: This typically covers a credit check and is not refundable. Sometimes landlords will also request a "good faith" deposit, which will go toward the first month's rent once your application is approved.

Cozy: Usually code for a tiny space.

Galley Kitchen: Generally found in smaller apartments, these kitchens have appliances and countertops that run parallel to each other, separated by a narrow walkway. Unlike an "eat-in" kitchen, there's usually no room for a table.

Garden Apartment: This is the basement unit, or the apartment underneath the parlor floor. It tends to be darker with lower ceilings, although many come with outdoor or "garden" access to the backyard.

Parlor Floor: The floor that the front door opens onto in a townhouse—technically the second floor, accessed by a set of stairs. This floor is traditionally the grandest and has the highest ceilings.

Half Bath: A bathroom with a toilet and sink but no bathtub or shower.

Junior One-Bedroom: Legally a bedroom needs to have a window, so this is technically a studio apartment with an additional small, windowless room.

Loft: A large open space with no walls and high ceilings that can be divided up or "converted" from a light industrial space into a residential unit.

Walk-Up: This means that there's no elevator, so think about how many flights of stairs you're willing to climb every day.

Stay on track. A traditional railroad apartment is long and narrow, where each room opens onto the next. Usually the rooms on either end are larger with windows while the middle rooms are smaller and darker. The way you use the space will help determine how you set it up—whether you want to use the bigger, brighter room as your bedroom or if you mind people walking through your sleeping area to get to the living room.

Extend your shelf life. Even a single plant adds personality to a space. It doesn't need to take up a lot of room—small dressers, side tables, and mantle tops offer the perfect perch. Choose pretty pots to add a sculptural element.

Go with the grain. Natural materials like wood bring warmth to a space and make it feel grounded. Small side tables instead of a large coffee table are easy to move around for overnight guests or morning workout sessions. A compact desk in the living room is all you need to set up a workspace. If you're a stickler for removing shoes near the entryway, place a bench there as a helpful reminder to others.

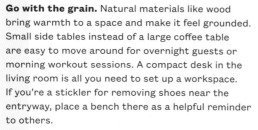

Budgeting

Make Your Money Count.

Determining your budget is a key first step. You might want a big kitchen for entertaining friends or to be in the newest loft, but if you don't have any money left after you've paid the rent, even the most luxurious space will become a burden. The standard rule is to spend no more than 30 percent of your net income on housing. Do the math before you make a commitment, and don't forget to add in moving costs like security deposit, first (and sometimes last) month's rent, renter's insurance, broker's fee, and movers. And keep in mind what your monthly bills and student loans will be.

Solo

Play with blocks. Construct a simple shelving unit with building materials like concrete blocks and sheets of plywood. You don't need nails or glue so it's easy to reconfigure or add on to as your space evolves.

No closet? Turn a small alcove into clothing storage with strategically placed shelves, rods, and chests. When it's open to the rest of the room, keeping things clean and organized is even more important.

Lessons in Layering

Thoughtfully arranged textiles, objects, and art make a room feel loved and lived-in. Pick a palette, experiment with contrasts, and try to keep a common thread running throughout so things feel cohesive instead of chaotic. Here's how to make the most of the mix.

Start with neutrals, then play with small splashes of color.

Walls and furniture in easy-to-live-with whites, grays, and ivories give you a versatile "blank canvas" to work with. Use accessories to give your space its personality. This low-commitment approach makes it easy to update your space's look whenever you want.

Put patterns on repeat. Using the same pattern in multiple places creates rhythm and movement in a room. To

keep all of the patterns from looking messy or monotonous, stick to a palette of two or three colors, then play with scale (bigger and smaller versions of the same print) and motifs (florals, stripes, and geometrics in the same tones).

Strike a balance.
Hard and soft, rough and smooth, old and new. Juxtapose contrasting textures to give a room depth and dimension.

Add vintage touches. A few old pieces automatically add warmth to a space and keep things from looking like a home decor showroom. Plus, yard sale finds are usually good deals.

Use bookshelves for more than books. Objects have stories, too. Books can look heavy when they're crammed in together. Mix vertical rows with horizontal stacks, and give them room to breathe by adding small sculptures, bowls, boxes, and other mementos.

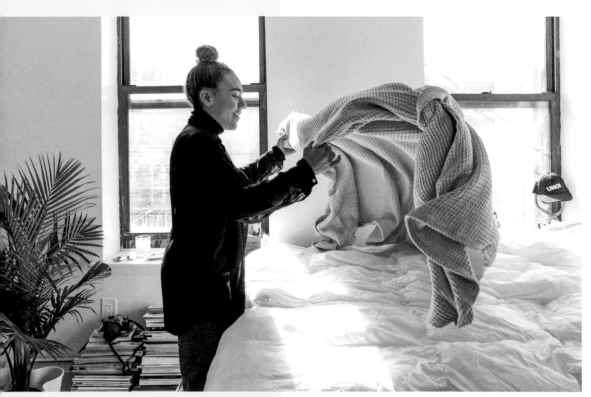

Organizing

Divide and Conquer.

In small apartments, resist the temptation to split a single room into separate mini rooms for dining, living, and sleeping. Instead, create more flexibility in one open space with adaptable pieces. You can even use rugs or large pieces of art to visually anchor different areas. For example, a small table can do triple duty as a nightstand, breakfast nook, and laptop workstation—and a sturdy futon full of pillows can be a place to lounge during the day and sleep at night.

Store more on the ground floor. Basements often don't have a lot of built-in storage so you'll have to improvise: use boxes and baskets stacked on open shelving to keep things together and out of site; consoles can hold everything from dishes and glasses to shoes and sweaters; and if you don't have a closet, a simple clothing rod is a lifesaver. Just remember: when everything is out in the open in a small studio, keeping things clean and tidy is more important than ever.

My Small Space

A Step-by-Step Floor Plan

While it's always smart to live in your apartment for a little while before making any big purchases, creating a floor plan is the best way to figure out what you have room for and how to lay it out. It's easy to move paper cutouts around, so let them do the heavy lifting before you start rearranging the furniture. Here's how to make sure everything fits.

Start by measuring your space. Include all doorways and windows to avoid blocking an entrance. It's also helpful to mark outlets and built-ins so you know exactly what you're working with.

Graph it out. Use quarter-inch graph paper to draw your room to scale, where a quarter-inch box equals one square foot.

Create to-scale paper furniture. Draw pieces on another sheet of graph paper, using the same quarter-inch-to-foot ratio. Then cut them all out like paper dolls.

Play with the pieces. Here's the fun part! Move them around and try different arrangements to see how pieces will fit together and what holes you need to fill.

Note spacing standards. Don't forget to allow for circulation around furniture and space in front of windows and doorways. Thirty to forty inches feels open enough for a main pathway, while eighteen inches between furniture lets people pass by.

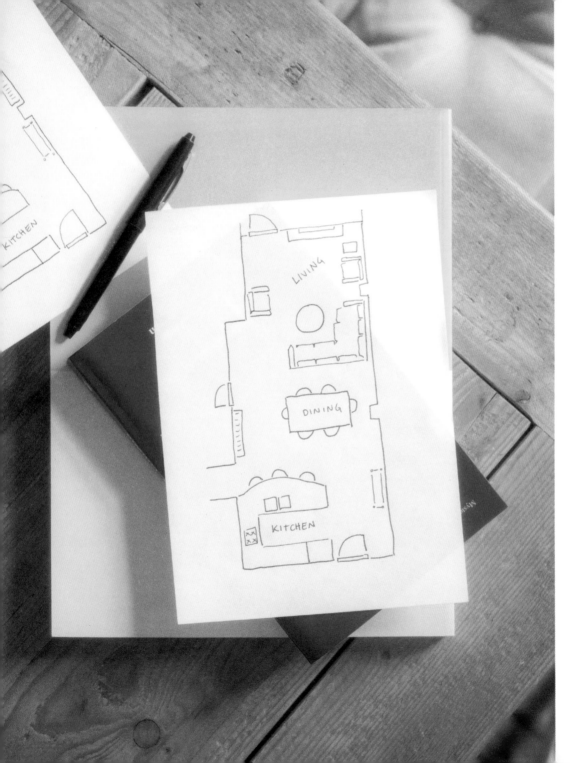

Art can be anything. Even if you can't afford a large framed piece, hanging less-expensive textiles can help ground a space, visually define an area, and set the room's palette. They're also a fun, low-commitment way to play with print. Try tapestries, fabric remnants, and small rugs.

It's All Yours.

One of the biggest challenges in a small space is to create flow and flexibility. Experiment with furniture in unexpected places— put a sofa in the middle of the room to separate your bed from the television, or use a bookshelf without a back to create an airy room divider. Once you have the big pieces in place, use throws, accent pillows, ceramics, and art to accessorize your small space in different ways. And change it up often until you land on a look you love.

Find a common thread. And weave it through your space. It can be any theme—such as a color, a pattern, or a recurring shape. Whatever it is, think about ways you can repeat it in different parts of your apartment. Maybe the bold color of a sofa shows up again in accent pieces such as a side table and throw pillows. Even if it's subtle, the effect will make your space feel pulled together and considered without looking cheesy or overly decorated.

Exhibit No. 1: The Gallery Wall

Art is a great way to inject color and personality into a room, but ultimately it should represent your tastes and unique style. There are many ways to arrange a collection, whether you have three pieces or twenty. Here's how to get that salon-style look.

Collect and curate.
Anything from postcards and personal photos to drawings and concert posters have visual impact. Print fairs, thrift shops, and flea markets are great places to start collecting. The most important rule is to pick pieces you love.

Frame it up.
A nice frame elevates even the simplest sketch but it's not always necessary to visit the frame shop—custom frames can be expensive, so reserve them for collectibles and heirlooms. It's fairly easy to find nice mat-ready frames for standard-size prints. Floating frames are a great option for inexpensive pieces like posters or homemade art. Ultimately, choose frames to suit the piece, not the space.

Find a focal point.
Pick one larger piece to anchor the collection. Then vary sizes and orientation. Smaller pieces are great for filling in odd spaces.

Make a plan.
To avoid putting unnecessary holes in the wall, it's safest to lay your composition on the floor ahead of time. Either snap a photo and use your eye to place pieces on the wall or make paper templates and tape them up to perfectly re-create your vision.

Space it right.
As a general guide, leave two to three inches between each piece to give your installation room to breathe.

Warm the House.

Just because your living room is also your bedroom doesn't mean you can't entertain. Sometimes such intimacy lends itself to more easygoing gatherings. However, when space is limited, be prepared for people to use every square inch. Cover your bed with thick blankets so your duvet doesn't get dirty when people sit on it, and line a few cushions up against the wall for guests to lean against. Making everyone comfortable is the key to a good party.

How to Host a Dinner Without a Dining Room

You don't need a table and fancy dishes to throw a great dinner party. Coffee and side tables can be surprisingly versatile. Think low-key vibes and low-slung seating. Without designated place settings, guests are free to mingle and move around. Here are a few tips to make sure everything goes smoothly.

Set up a help-yourself bar. Pre-batch a cocktail, open the wine, and put out a bottle of whiskey or a digestif for after-dinner drinks. Don't forget to include a few bottles of sparkling water for any nondrinkers. And make sure you have fresh ice and a bowl of presliced citrus garnishes.

Don't play with knives. Serve food that can be nibbled like bread and cheese, or create a buffet-like spread, such as a taco bar, where nothing needs to be cut. With limited elbow room and table space, extra silverware just gets in the way.

Make a playlist. Choose songs that keep the momentum up. Set the volume high enough to feel festive but not so loud that it makes it impossible to have a conversation. Try to add enough songs to last the length of the party so you don't have to think about it once guests arrive.

Use mismatched plates and glasses. This way you don't need to have complete sets and guests won't lose track of their dish.

Add a few floor pillows. Use soft cushions and folded-up blankets as extra seating when you don't have enough chairs.

Dial down the decorations. Seasonal flowers and votives sprinkled around are enough to make things feel warm and inviting.

Make an entrance—or an exit. If you don't have a hall or designated entryway, a few hanging hooks for coats and jackets, as well as a small ledge with a bowl where you can throw your keys, are all you really need when you're coming and going. Hanging a mirror is another great trick for opening up a small area and for that last look.

Resources

Accessories. It's nice to collect objects and decorative accessories over time. Look for unique items when you travel or things that have special meaning.

Antiques. There are good deals at local charity shops, Craigslist, and online auctions like eBay and LiveAuctioneers. If you find something you love that's not local, uShip will let you list items so drivers can bid on the delivery cost.

Art. 20x200, Society 6, Art.com, and Saatchi Art all offer affordable prints. If you want something framed, note standard sizes as custom frames can be quite expensive.

Bedding. Thread counts can be deceiving. Make sure sheets are woven from a quality, breathable material like pima cotton or linen and check whether they're single- or double-ply.

Furniture. Vintage pieces tend to be more affordable (and sustainable)—or get creative and build something simple: sawhorses and a piece of plywood for a table or stacking boxes for shelves and side tables.

Paint. Most hardware stores carry at least one major brand like Benjamin Moore or Sherwin-Williams. Paints have strong odors and can release low-level toxins. Consider low-VOC and eco-friendly options.

Plants. Hardware stores and local nurseries are good places to start. Online shops like Bloomscape and The Sill will deliver houseplants straight to your door.

Rugs. Look at home goods stores like West Elm, Crate & Barrel, Urban Outfitters, and IKEA for affordable options.

Window Treatments. Curtains can be made simply by attaching clip rings to a loose piece of fabric. Home improvement stores like Home Depot carry some affordable blind and shade options.

Acknowledgments

These photos began as a collaboration with the team at Urban Outfitters Home. Many of the apartments and dorms in this book feature the brilliance of their art direction and styling—especially that of John Murphy, Jenna Yankun, and Kelsi Windmiller. Their vision enhanced the existing personal style of each subject's home, highlighting their individuality. Thank you for asking me to collaborate with you. My thanks also go to Urban's former book buyer, Sara Neville, who conceptualized this project with my editor, Angelin Borsics. We all wanted to create an inspiring design book featuring unique subjects who found creative solutions within smaller spaces.

I want to thank everyone who opened their doors to me: Adrienne Raquel, Alayna Giovannitti, Alexis Jesup, Arpana Rayamjhi, Casey Zhang, Elise Peterson, Emilia + Amanda, Haley Stark, Ian Durkin, Kiersten Marian, Louise Hayat-Camard, Marcus Lloyd, Michael Clarke, Michael Hogan, Myles Loftin, Paloma Gil, R'el Dade, Rachael Yaeger, Rockie Nolan, Ryan Natsis, Spencer Richardson, Tanisha Pina, Tess Orgasan, Timothy Mahoney, and Viktoria Dahlberg.

This book would not be possible without the help of my writer, Chloe Lieske, who brought her expertise in the subject of interior design to each photograph. Many thanks as well to my editor, Andrea Bussell, for her discerning eye and her patience.

A warm thanks to the team at Clarkson Potter for asking me to take part in this project and to Angelin Borsics for leading the way. Thank you to designer Ian Dingman; production manager Heather Williamson; production editor Terry Deal; and managing editor Aislinn Belton.

And thank you to my father, who always lent a helping hand when I was rearranging furniture for the third time that month or asking to repaint my bedroom for the second time that year. I inherited my dedication to photography and design from him.

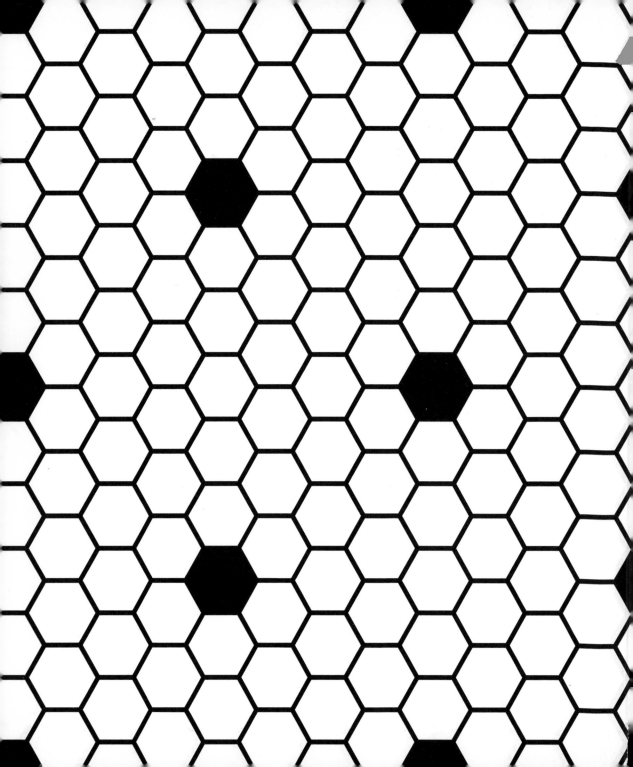